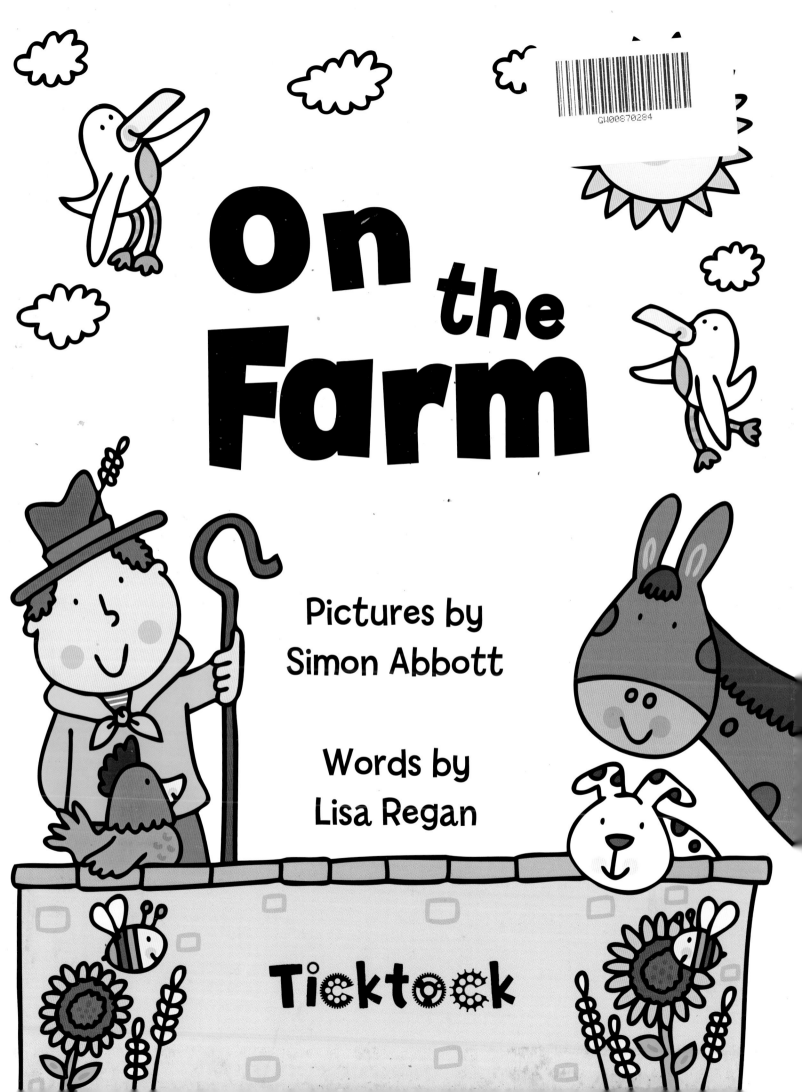

On the Farm

Pictures by
Simon Abbott

Words by
Lisa Regan

Ticktock

Here We Grow

Without farms, we wouldn't have much to eat! Many farmers grow plants in their fields, which we then use for food. These types of plants are called crops.

Crops include grains such as **wheat** and **barley** which are used to make **bread** and **breakfast cereals**.

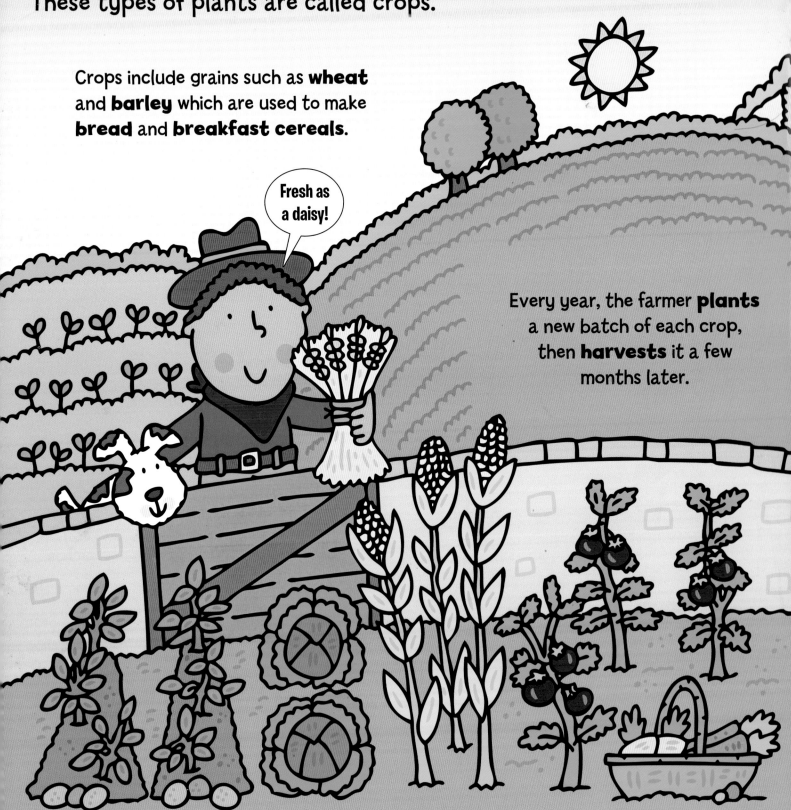

Fresh as a daisy!

Every year, the farmer **plants** a new batch of each crop, then **harvests** it a few months later.

Lots of farmers also grow different **vegetables** and **fruits**, such as potatoes, sweetcorn, cabbages and tomatoes.

Sometimes, farmers spray crops with chemicals (called **pesticides**) to stop insects eating them.

Farmers use **tractors** to do many jobs. A tractor can plough a field (turn over the soil), rake the ground, and move heavy objects.

Let's get bizzzzy!

Bees are important to farmers as they spread **pollen** from plant to plant, which helps them grow.

Animal Farm

Farmers raise many different kinds of animals - not just for food, but for materials such as wool and leather.

Farm birds - chickens, ducks, turkeys and geese - are called **poultry**. They are kept for their eggs and meat, and sometimes for their feathers.

NO FOXES!

Cock-a-doodle-doo!

Egg-cellent!

Once they are laid, duck and goose eggs are often hatched **by chickens**. The farmer uses chickens because they are more likely to sit on the eggs and not wander off!

FUN FACTS

Animal skins can be dried to make leather and used for clothes, shoes, bags and furniture.

In some countries, **crocodiles** and **alligators** are farmed for their meat and skin.

Lots of other animals are kept on farms, such as
yaks, llamas, goats, ostriches, buffalo, deer and rabbits.

Sheep grow a thick woolly coat that can be clipped off each year –
called **shearing** – and this is turned into wool.

Silkworms
(a kind of caterpillar)
are kept in farms to
produce thread to make silk.

In **New Zealand**,
there are seven
times more sheep
than people!

Have You Herd?

Farmers can keep cows for their milk. Other farmers raise animals, including cows, sheep and pigs, for their meat.

A cow eats about **70 kilograms of grass** each day. That's the same as 80 lettuces!

Moo-ve along now!

A large group of farm animals is called a **herd**. Some farmers keep over 1,000 cows or sheep!

FUN FACTS

In many countries, **guinea pigs** are kept as pets, but in South America they are raised for their meat!

Come and get them!

SPECIAL OFFER

The meat from a cow is called **beef** and the meat from a sheep is called **lamb**. Some people eat deer meat, which is called **venison**.

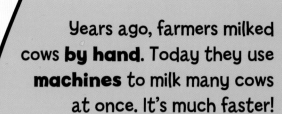

Years ago, farmers milked cows **by hand**. Today they use **machines** to milk many cows at once. It's much faster!

Even using machines, it takes nearly ten minutes to milk a cow.

My milk's udder-ly delicious!

When sheep and cows eat grass, they swallow it then **burp** it back up to chew again.

Disgusting!

It's been proven that **playing music** to cows helps them relax and produce more milk!

WOW!

Small Scale

Not all farmers sell the things they produce. Sometimes they only have enough to feed their own family.

Small farms aren't large enough for big machines. The farmers still dig the soil with **tools**, and sow the seeds by **hand**.

I'm digging this, man!

A small farm needs to grow as many useful crops as possible. In Africa, farmers grow food that contains lots of goodness and fills you up, such as **yams**, **cassava**, **sweet potatoes** and **beans**.

Goats are a very useful farm animal. They eat just about anything, even berries high on trees, and in return provide **milk**, **meat** and **skins**.

A **shepherd** is a person who takes care of sheep. They often live alongside their animals, high up in the mountains where the sheep graze.

Farmers that move from place to place are called **nomads**. They usually live in poorer countries, and travel with their herds to find new food for the animals.

Did You Know?
There are around **1,000** different types of sheep.

Goats can **jump** high enough to leap right over your head!

WOW!

Llama and yak farmers collect their animals' **droppings** to burn as **fuel**!

Toasty!

Big Business

Some farms are enormous - bigger than half a million football pitches. They sell everything they produce to supermarkets or big companies.

A large farm full of animals is often called a **ranch**. The animals kept there, usually cows, wander for miles grazing on the land.

Let's round 'em up!

Cowboys look after the roaming cows, called **cattle**. Traditionally they herd them on horseback but some modern cowboys use **quad bikes** and even **helicopters**!

FUN FACTS

A single dairy cow can produce **4,000 litres of milk** each year.

In Australia and New Zealand, cowboys are called 'jackaroos'.

Large areas of **rainforest** have been cleared to make way for big farms, but this is harmful to our planet, because trees produce **oxygen** that we need to breathe.

This is the last straw!

Big farms use gigantic machines to produce lots of crops. They are **expensive**, so sometimes farmers share them with each other.

Many different kinds of things are produced on large farms, not just vegetables, dairy and meat. In hot countries, farmers produce **bananas, rubber, cotton, tea, coffee, sugarcane** and **rice.**

There are five types of corn, but only one of them explodes well enough to make **popcorn.**

I'm ready to pop!

WOW!

Marvellous Machines

In the past, farmers dug, planted, fed, watered and harvested their fields by hand. Today, many farmers use machines to do all of these jobs more easily.

A **combine harvester** does three jobs in one go. It **cuts** the corn, **loosens** the seeds, and **leaves behind** the dry stalks.

All in a day's work!

The stalks that are left on the field are called **straw.** A machine collects the stalks and squashes them into large bales to be used for **animal bedding**.

FUN FACTS

Milking machines can get **400 glasses** of milk each day from just one cow!

Slurp!

One tractor used for pulling heavy machinery is as strong as **300 horses!**

Crops are sprayed using machines. Many farmers use a trailer with long arms which shoot out liquid to the plants. Some farmers use a **plane**, squirting the crops from high above! The liquid helps to control weeds, insects and plant diseases, and stop the crops growing too tall.

Combine harvesters have a **satnav** to guide them so they can work in the dark.

Turn left at the next hedge...

Some big dairy farms have a machine to turn **cow poo** into a gas. The gas is used to power another machine, called a generator, that makes **electricity**.

The **biggest tractor tyres** are over 2 metres tall - higher than the door of a house!

WOW!

From Harvest to Home

Growing crops and raising animals is just the first step in producing food for us to eat. It also needs to be harvested, processed and packaged.

Fruit is usually **harvested by hand** - it is hard to pick with machines as it is soft and easy to damage.

Gently does it.

To make **bread**, grains of wheat are ground (squashed) into **flour** and then baked in loaves.

Milk is turned into other foods, like **butter**, **cheese** and **yogurt**. Cheese is often made from the milk of cows, sheep or goats but can come from more than 20 different animals, including buffaloes!

Factories turn a single crop into many different foods. **Potatoes** can be put in tins, cooked into **crisps**, or turned into **chips**, **waffles**, **mash** or **hash browns**!

One potato... two potato...

Vegetables have to be processed quickly, before they go bad. They are **kept cold** and put in packets, ready to be sold in shops.

This one's for the chop!

A Day with the Animals

Farmers who raise animals have to work very hard. They have to get up early in the morning and work long days.

The farming day begins when the **sun rises**. The farmer feeds the animals and checks that they aren't ill or injured. A farmer will be able to tell if any are pregnant and keep a close eye on them.

Dairy cows are herded to the **milking shed**. They go back to the fields when they have been milked.

After milking, the farmer checks that the animals have plenty to eat. In **winter**, if there is not enough grass, they are given grass that's been stored since the summer.

FUN FACTS

Horses are most likely to have their babies, called **foals**, at night.

A healthy **lamb** will stand up and walk just a **few minutes** after it's born.

In the evening, the farmer will do **indoor jobs**, like phoning the vet and paying bills to keep the farm running smoothly.

The farmer has lots more jobs to do after lunch. This is when things can be **cleaned**, **built** or **mended**, such as fences, buildings, tractors and other machinery.

It's all go!

Often the farmer will travel around the farm on a small **quad bike** instead of a big tractor – it's easier, quicker and cheaper!

A farmer blindfolds **ostriches** to keep them calm when moving or examining them.

Often cows will **poo** on the farmer's head when they're fixed into the milking machine!

WOW!

In the Fields

No matter what they're growing, farmers must look after the crops and land the whole year round. It's a big job! Here's what a rice farmer has to do:

Rice is the second biggest crop in the world, after **maize**. For many people across the globe, rice makes up the main part of their diet.

Rice is grown in **paddy fields**. These fields are often found on steep hillsides. To be able to grow rice in such an awkward place, the farmer must create big, flat steps in the land. Before planting the seeds, the farmer will add **fertilizer** and make grooves in the soil for the seeds to sit in.

I've got soggy toes!

The farmer **soaks** the rice seeds in water and then plants them. Water is poured onto the fields until they are **flooded**, then the shoots gradually appear.

Fun Farm Facts

Bees are often attracted to flowers of just one colour, leaving the other flowers for different bees.

Some farms are very wet: **fish farms**! Enormous tanks are filled with fish such as salmon and carp.

Farming first began around **12,000** years ago!

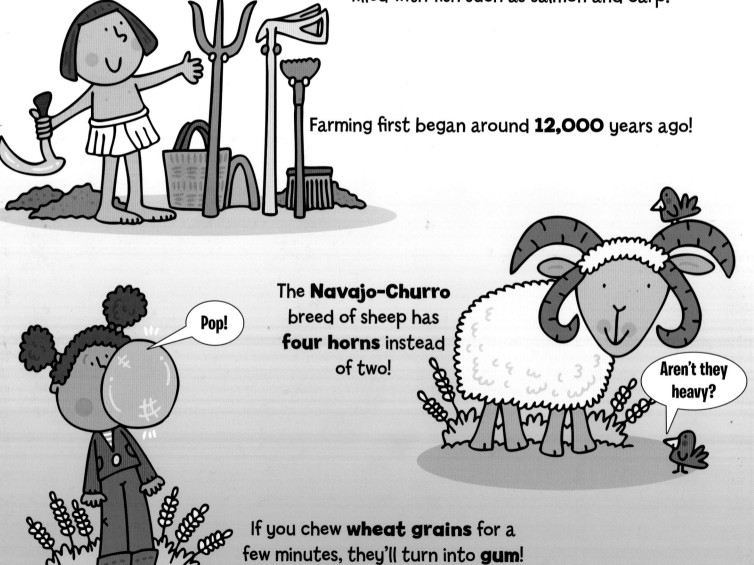

The **Navajo-Churro** breed of sheep has **four horns** instead of two!

If you chew **wheat grains** for a few minutes, they'll turn into **gum**!